Notes

A colouring book with simplified indigounous designs, accompanied by Ojibwe and English words to assist in learning about Ojibwe names for different mammals and plants.

For more information on how to pronounce individual words please refer to The Ojibwe People's Dictionary at https://ojibwe.lib.umn.edu/

Copyright © 2020 by Kendra L. Howland

This book belongs to Kendra L. Howland. You may use the designs and illustrations for educational graphics and crafts applications, free and without special permission, provided that you include no more than four in the same publication or project. (For permission for additional use, please write to kendrahowland.publications@gmail.com) However, republication or reproduction of any illustration by any other graphic service, whether it be in a book or in any other design resource, is strictly prohibited.

Amik

Beaver

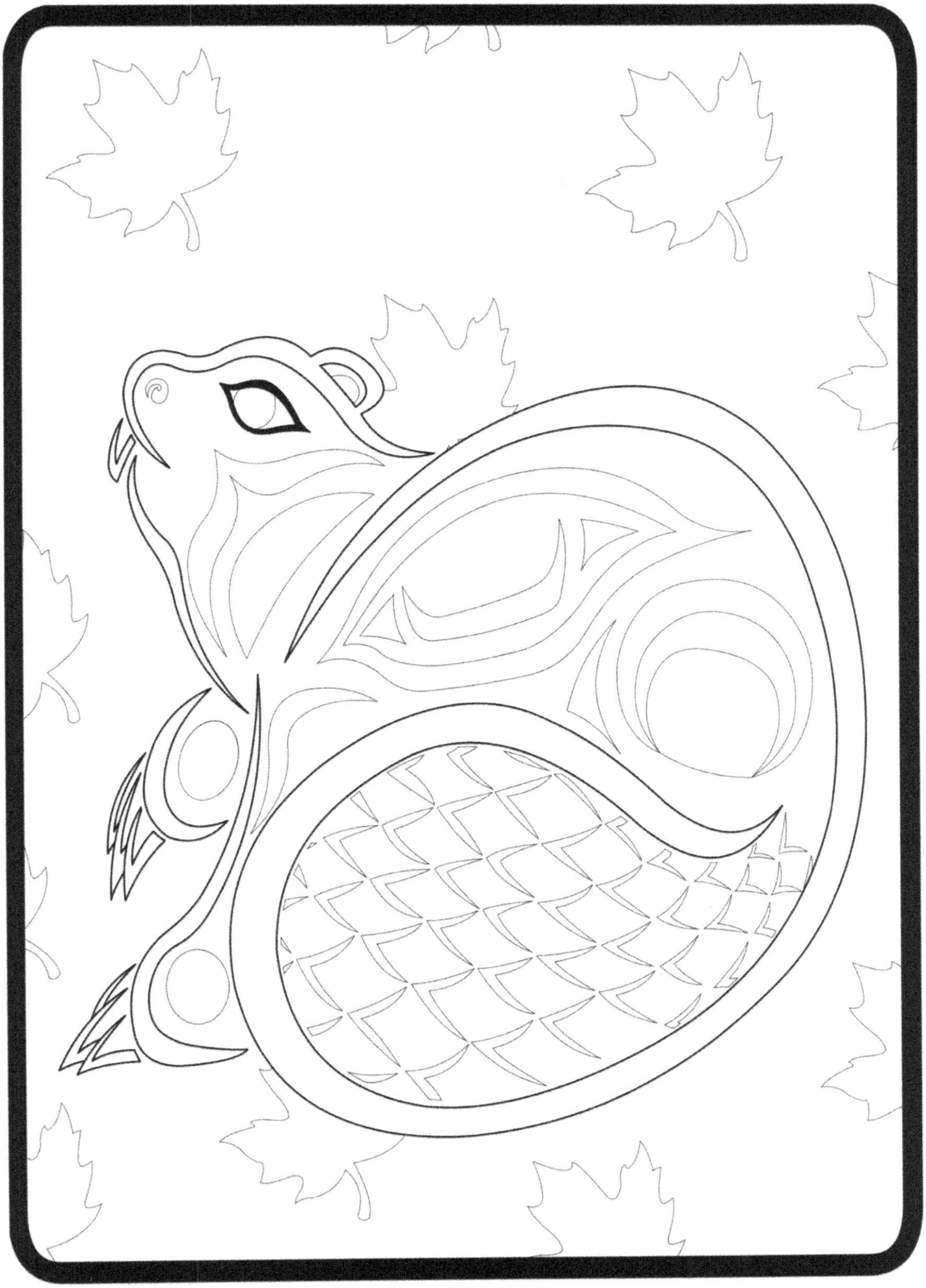

Ma'iingan

Wolf

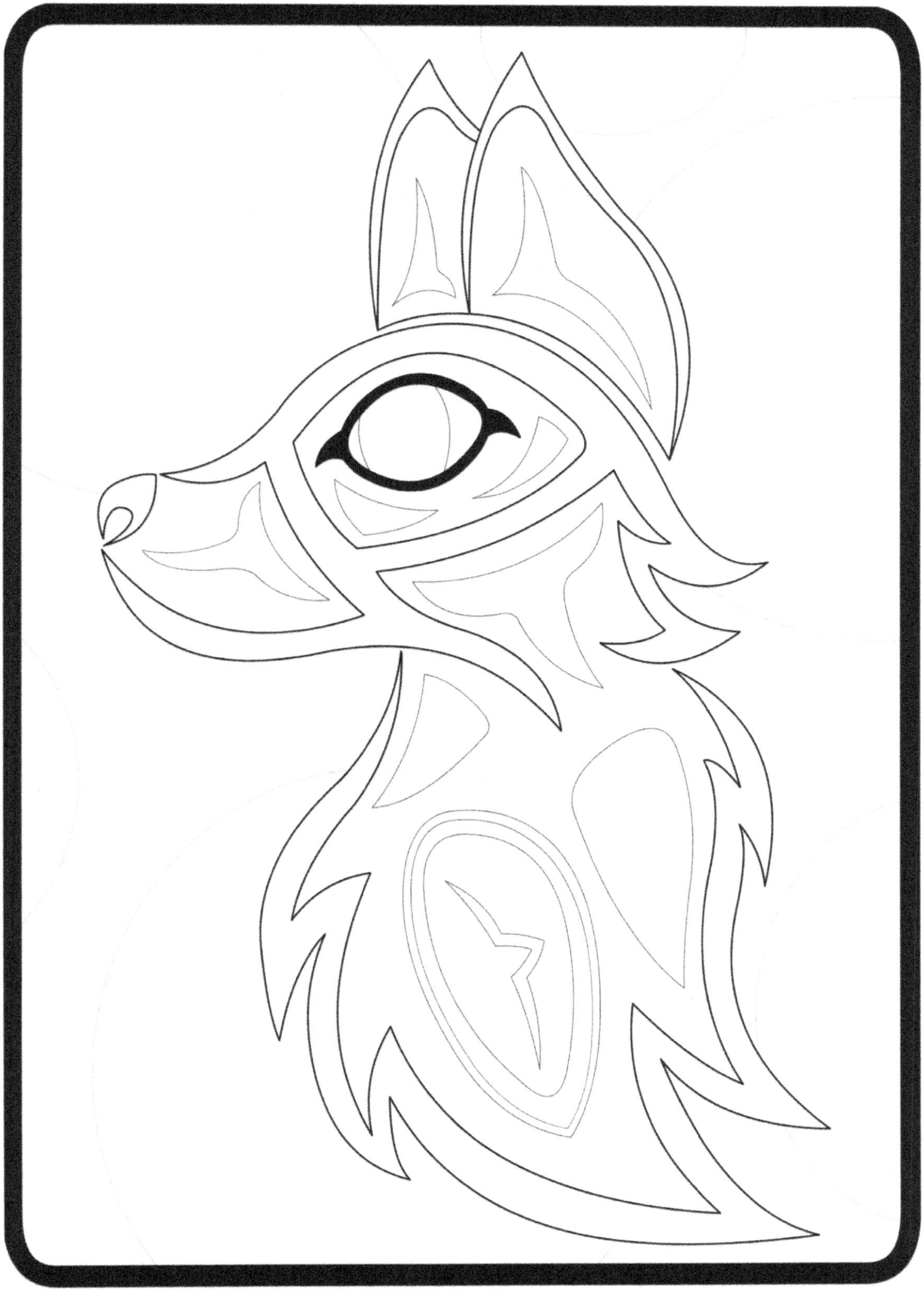

Mishibizhii

Mountain Lion

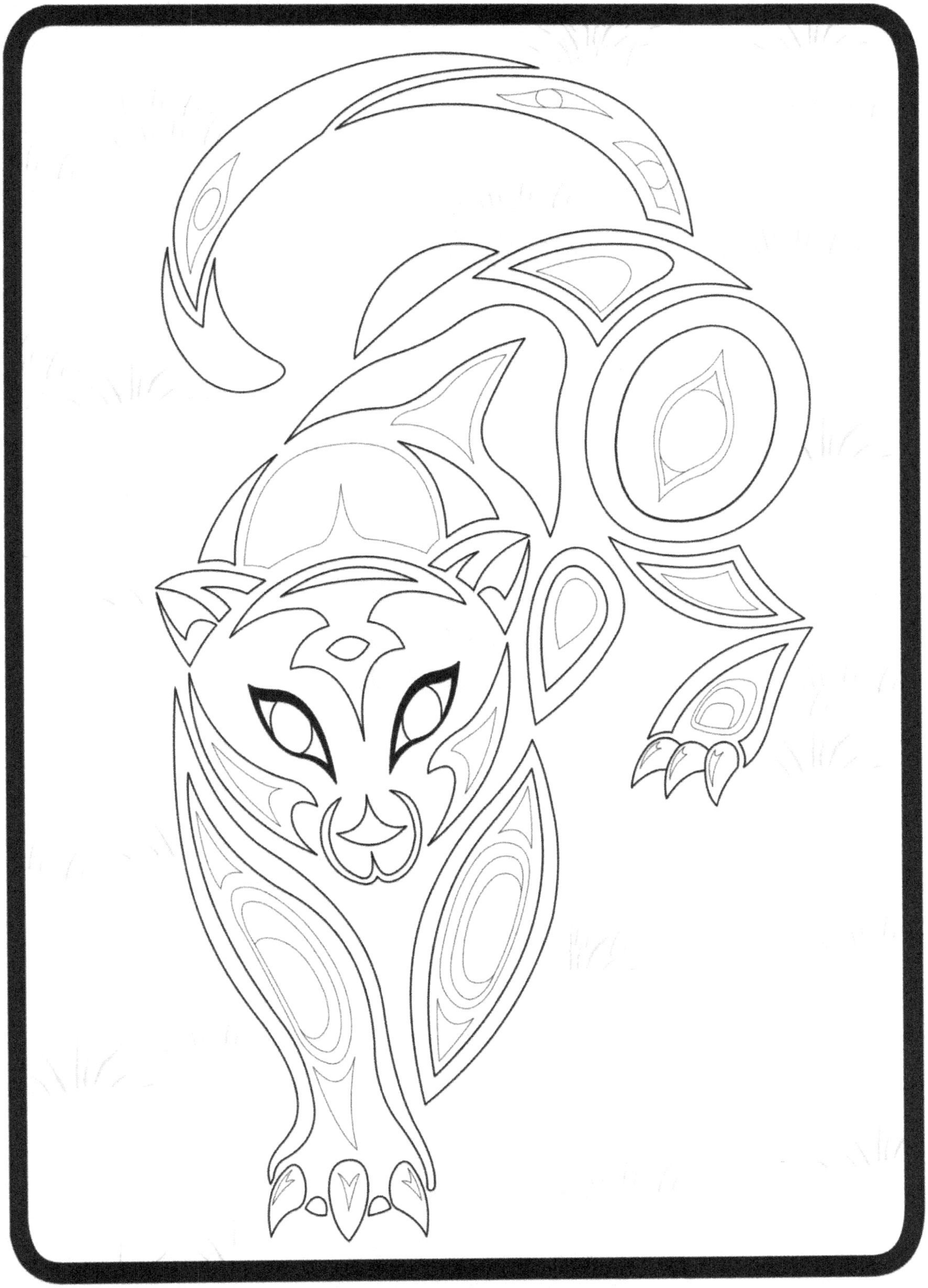

Waagosh

Fox

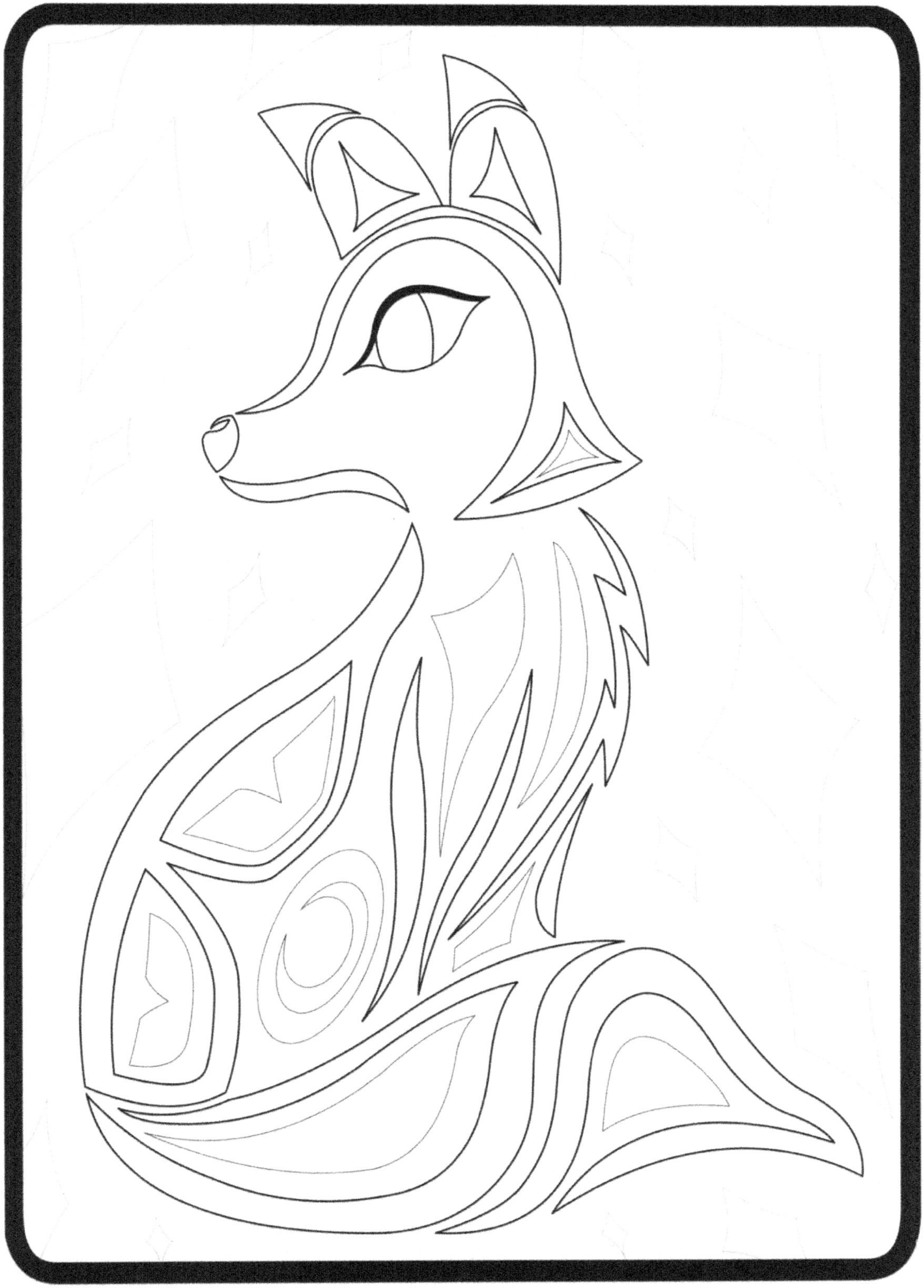

Esiban

Raccoon

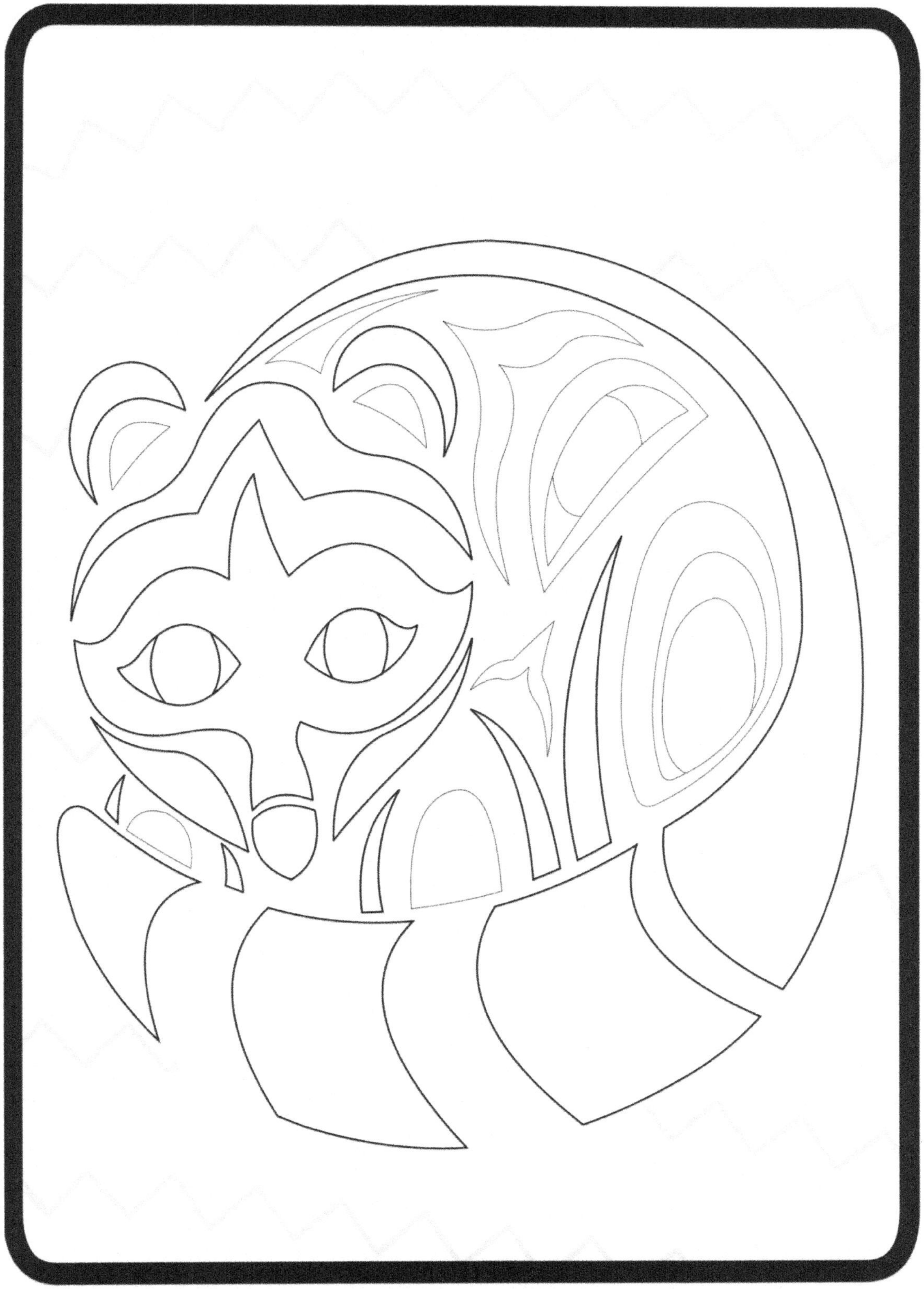

Waabooz

Rabbit

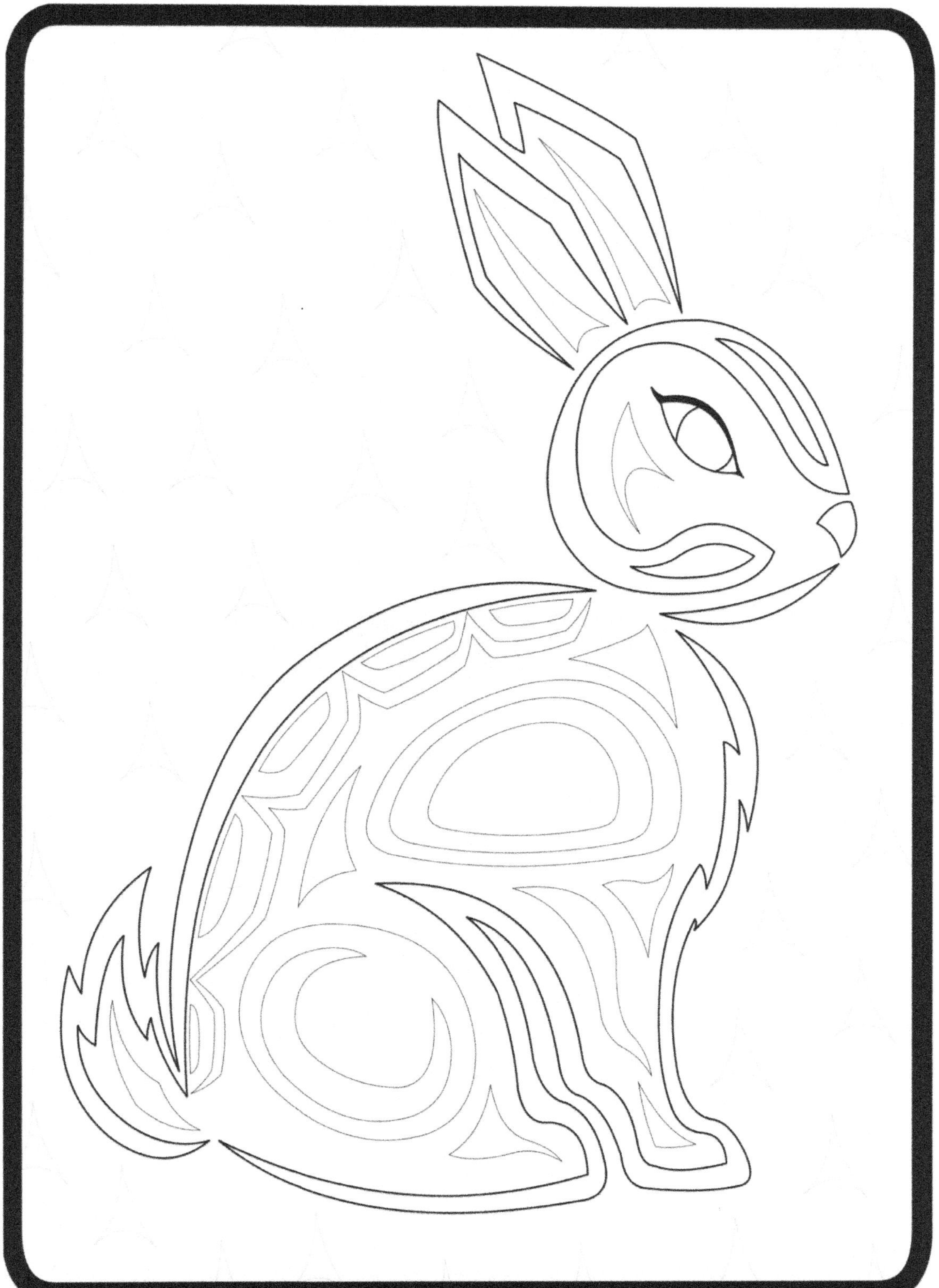

Ajidamoo

Squirrel

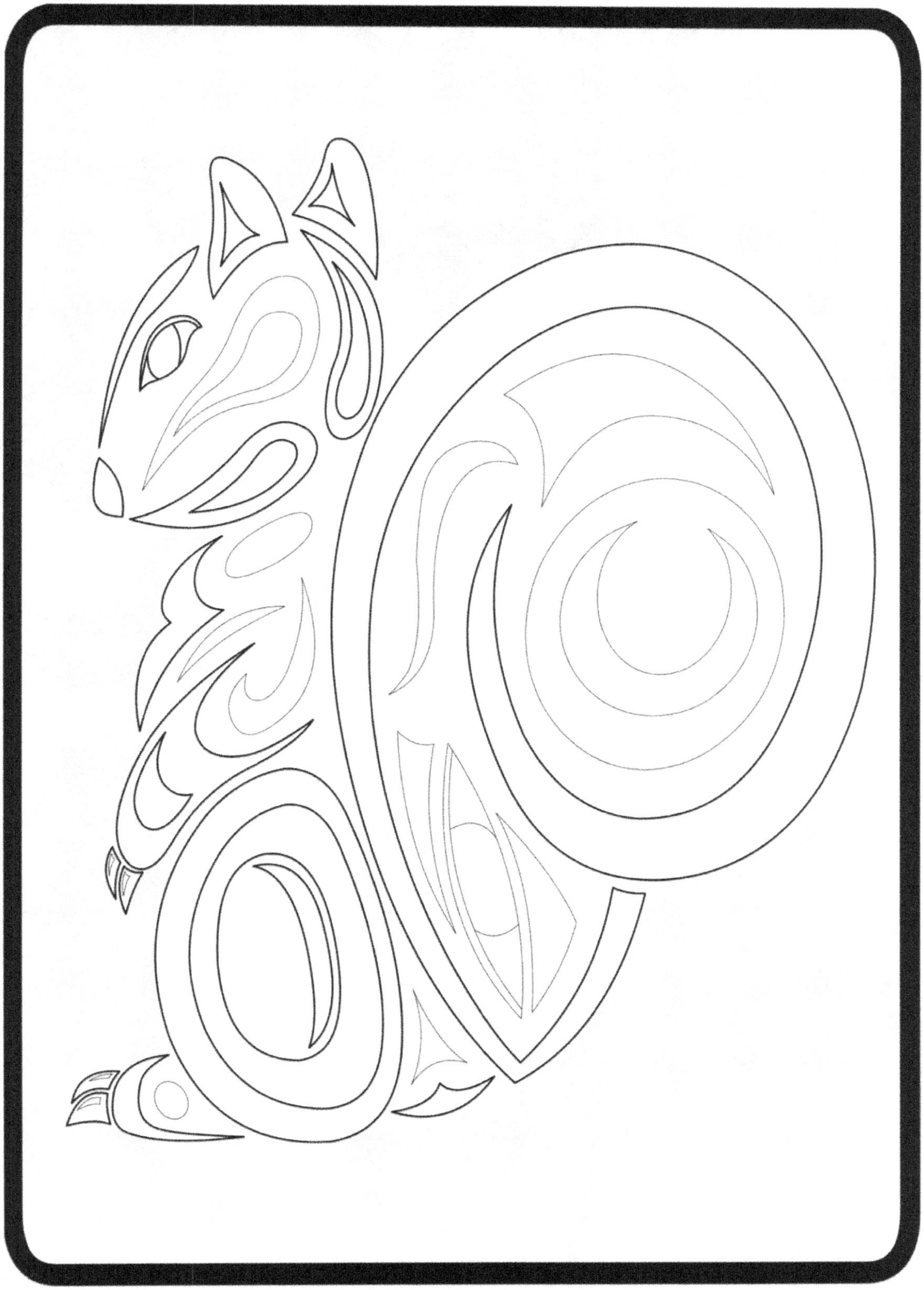

Nigig

Otter

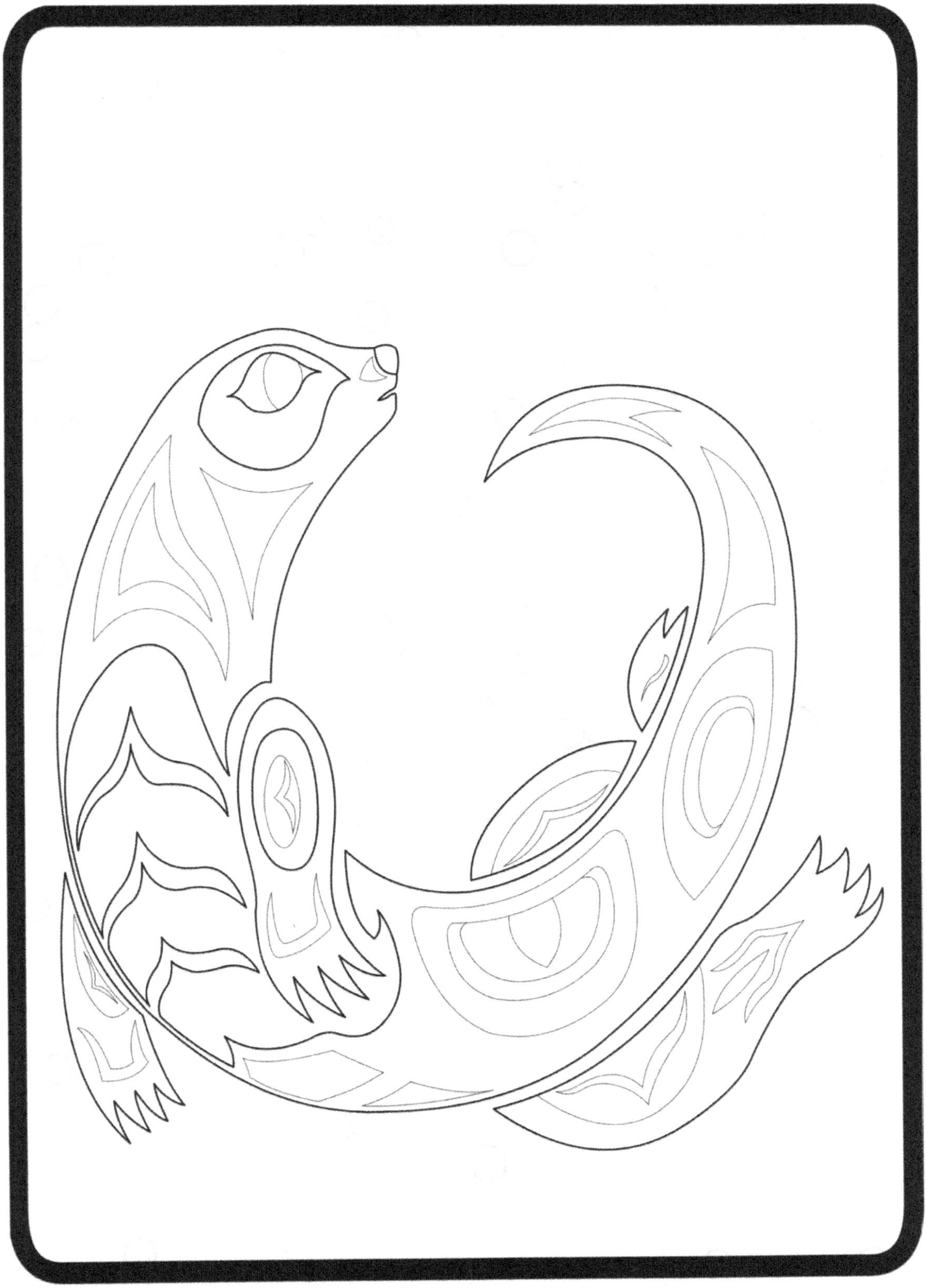

Mikinaak

Snapping Turtle

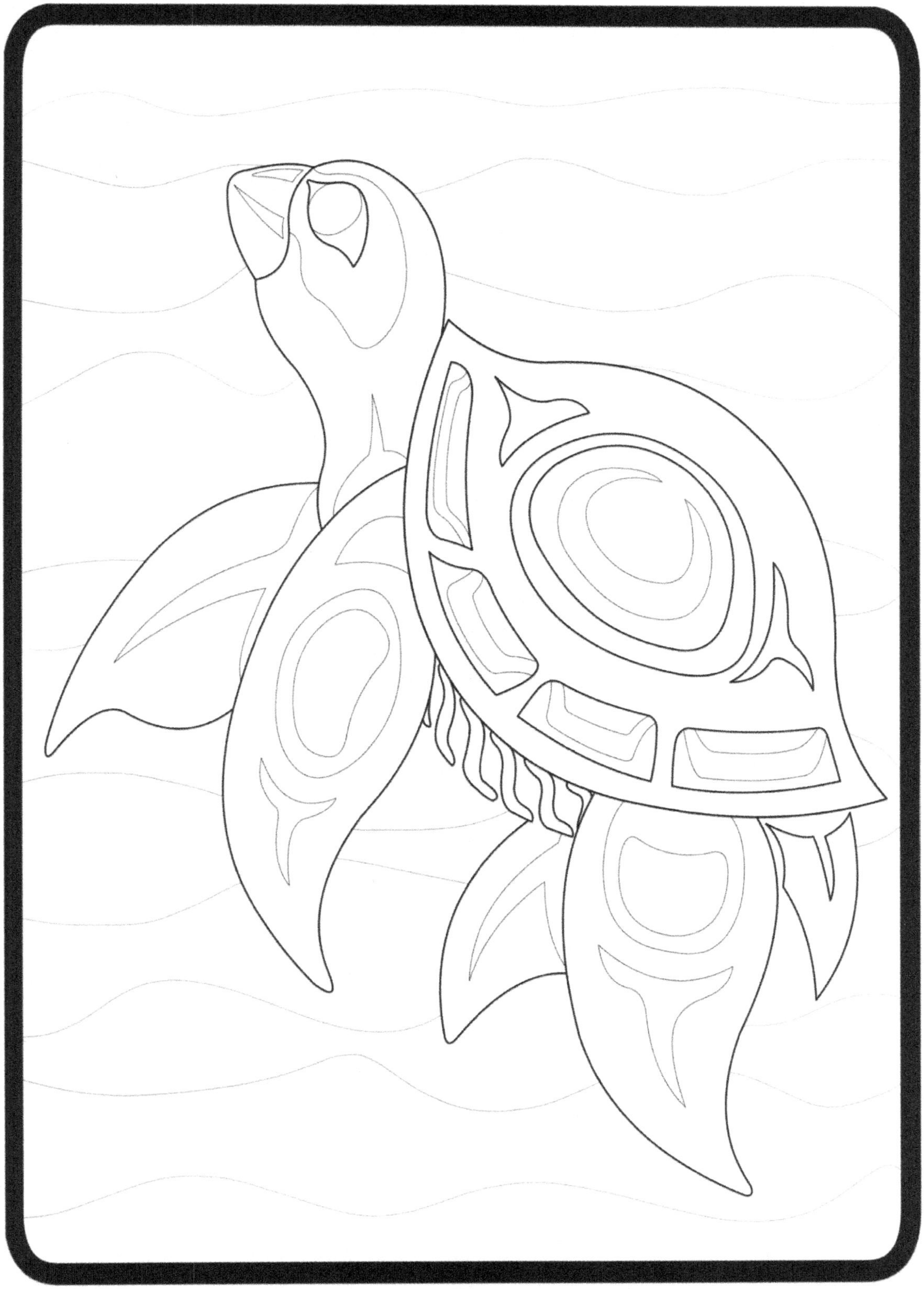

Orca

Orca

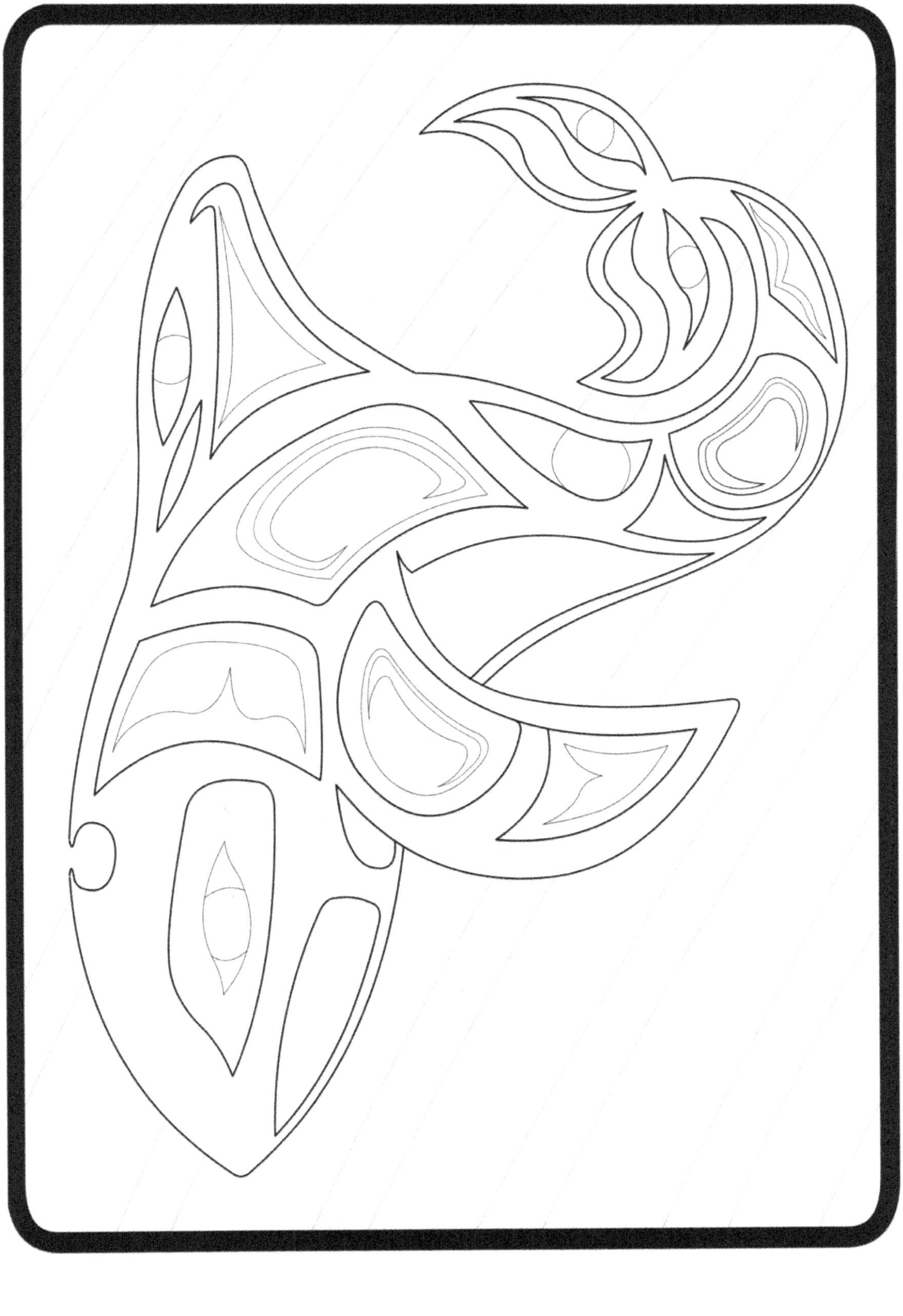

Gitchie Manameg

Whale

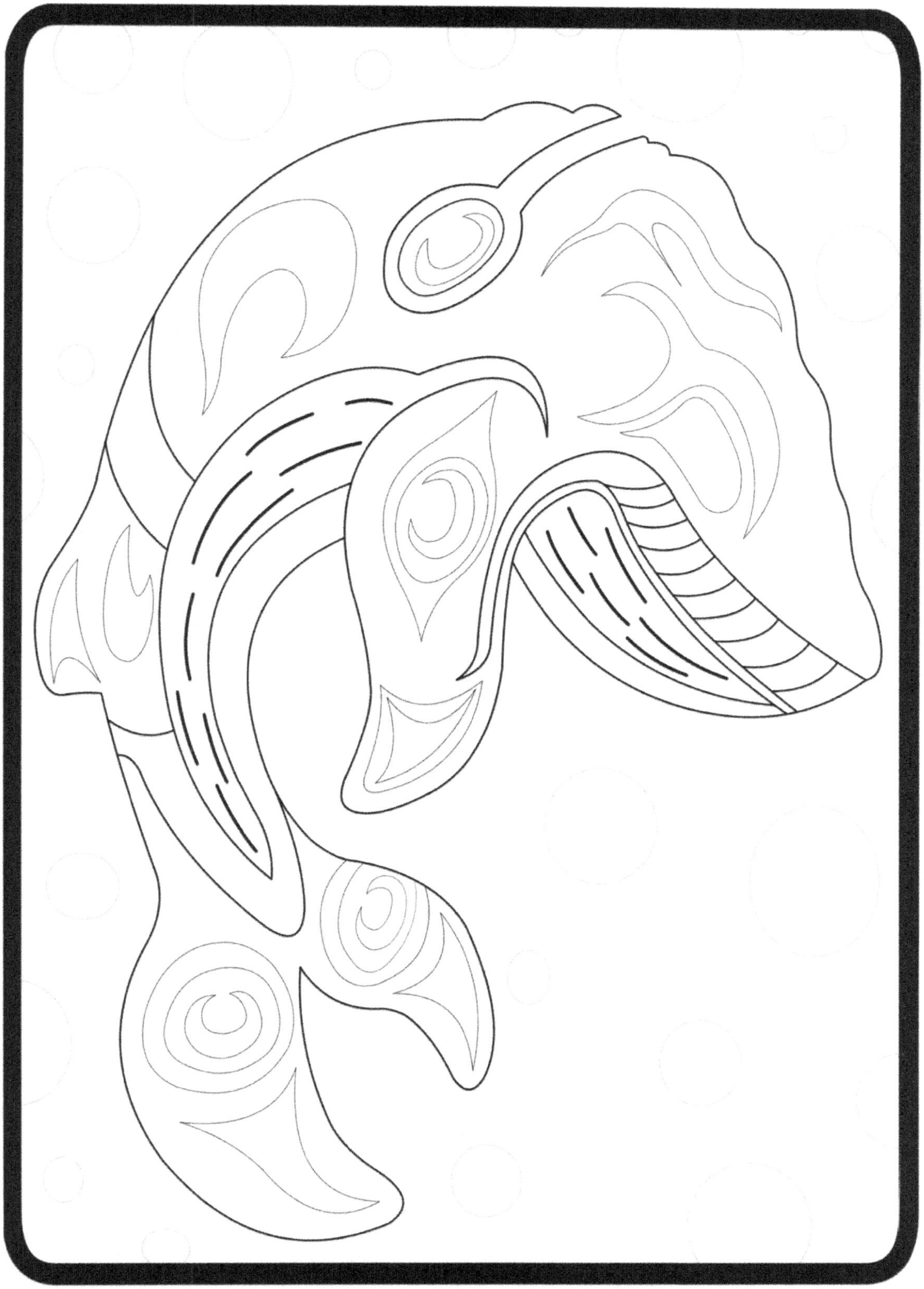

Waabizii

Swan

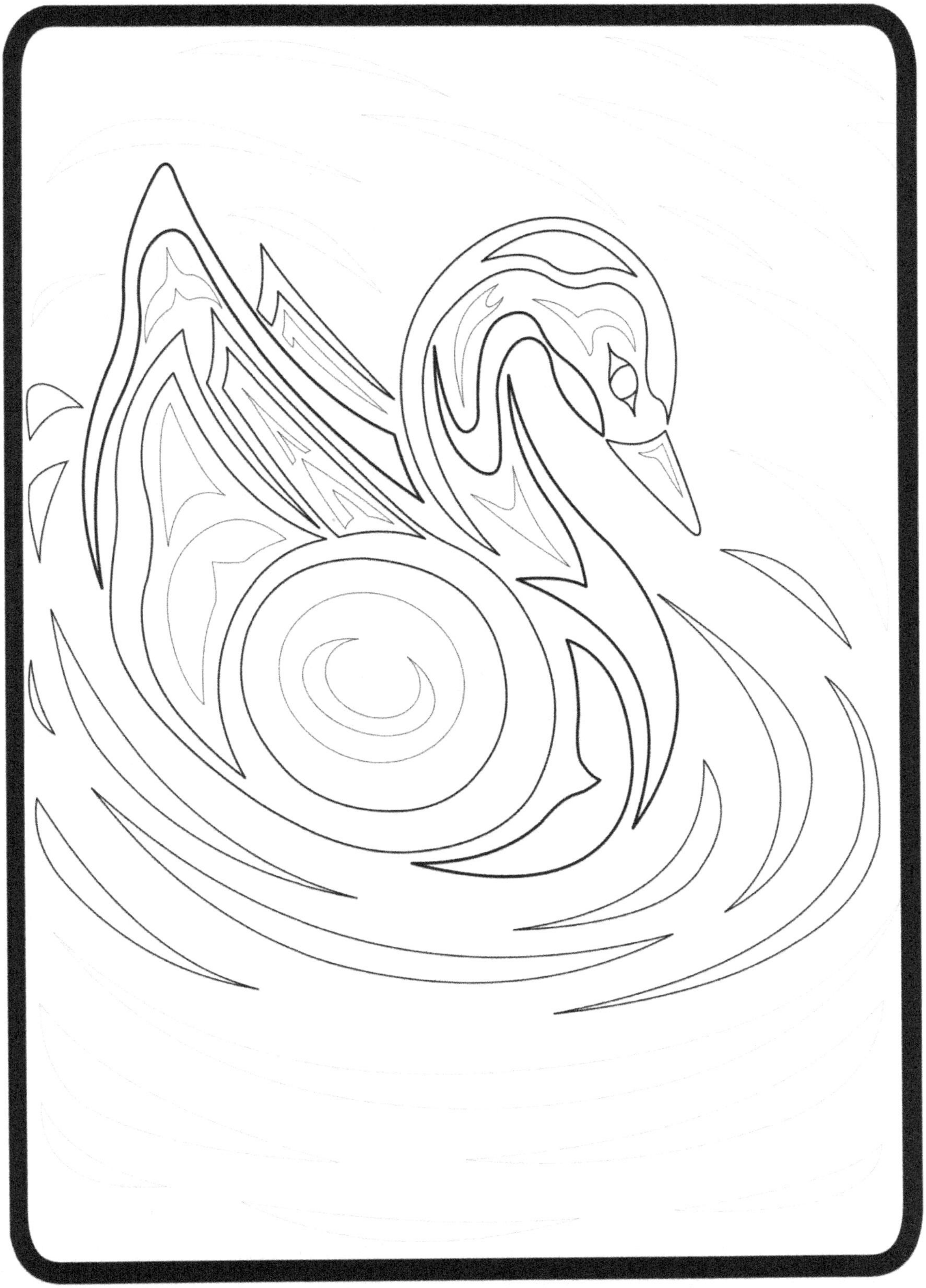

Maang

Loon

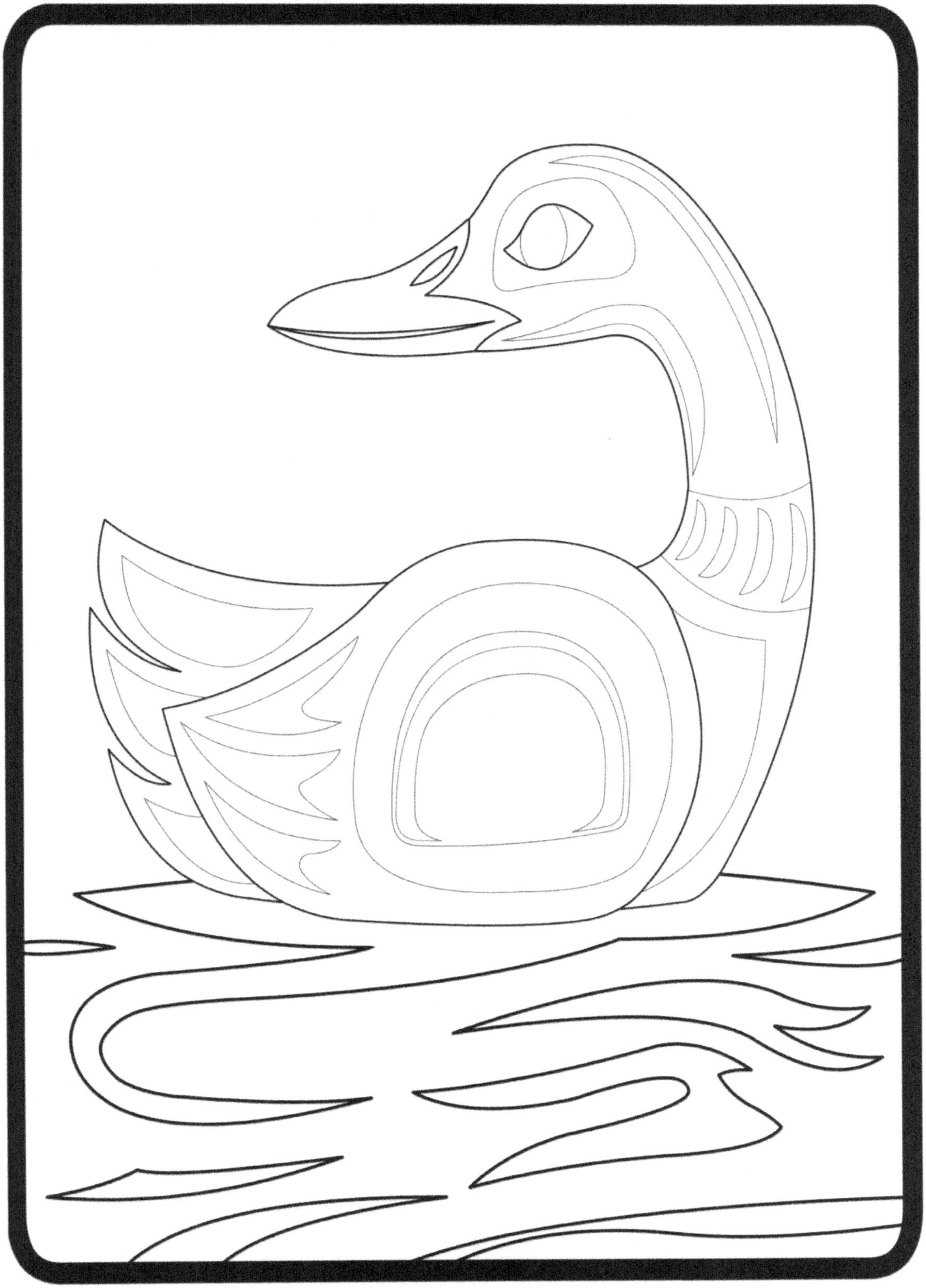

Zhiishiib

Duck

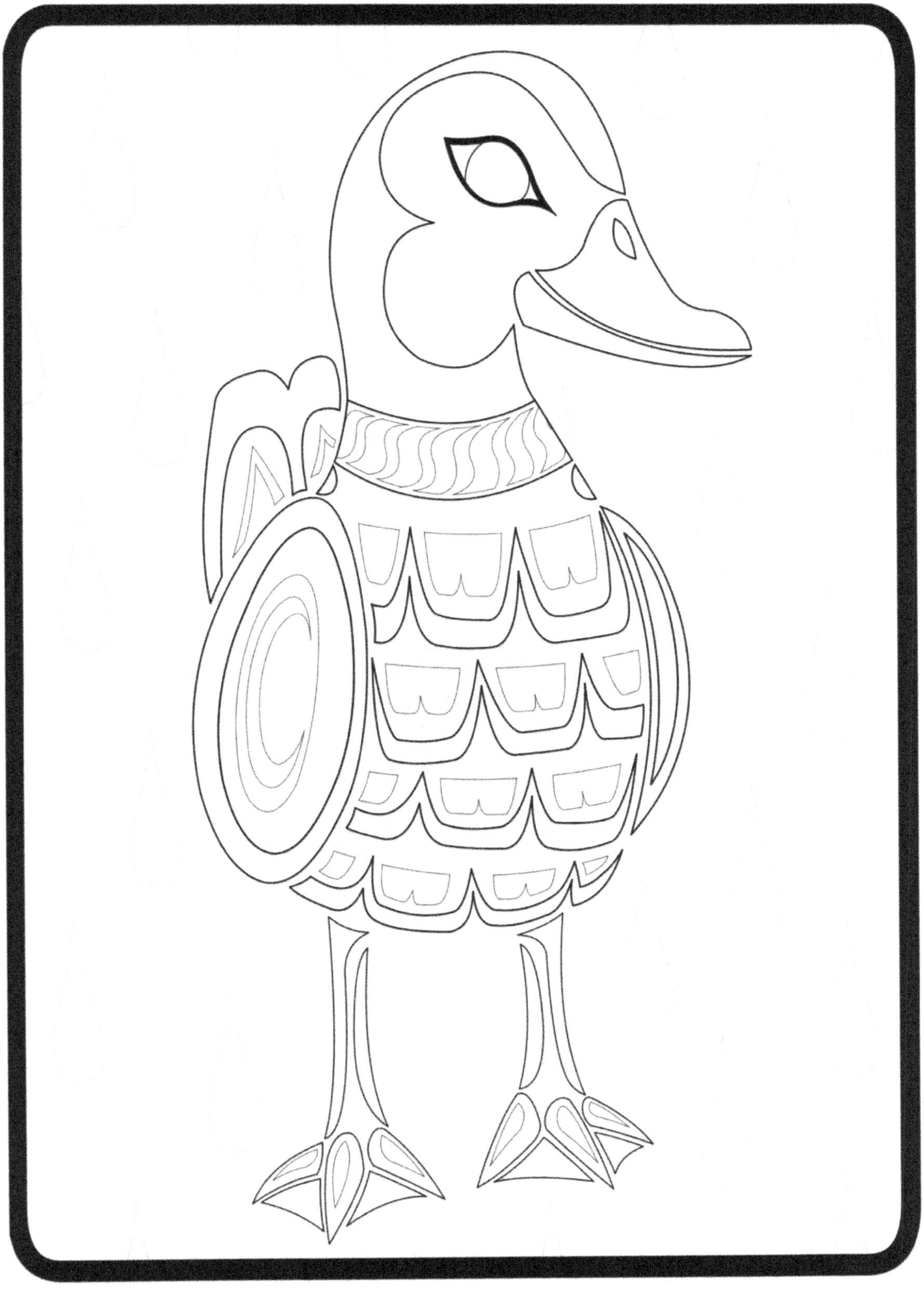

Nenookaasi

Humming Bird

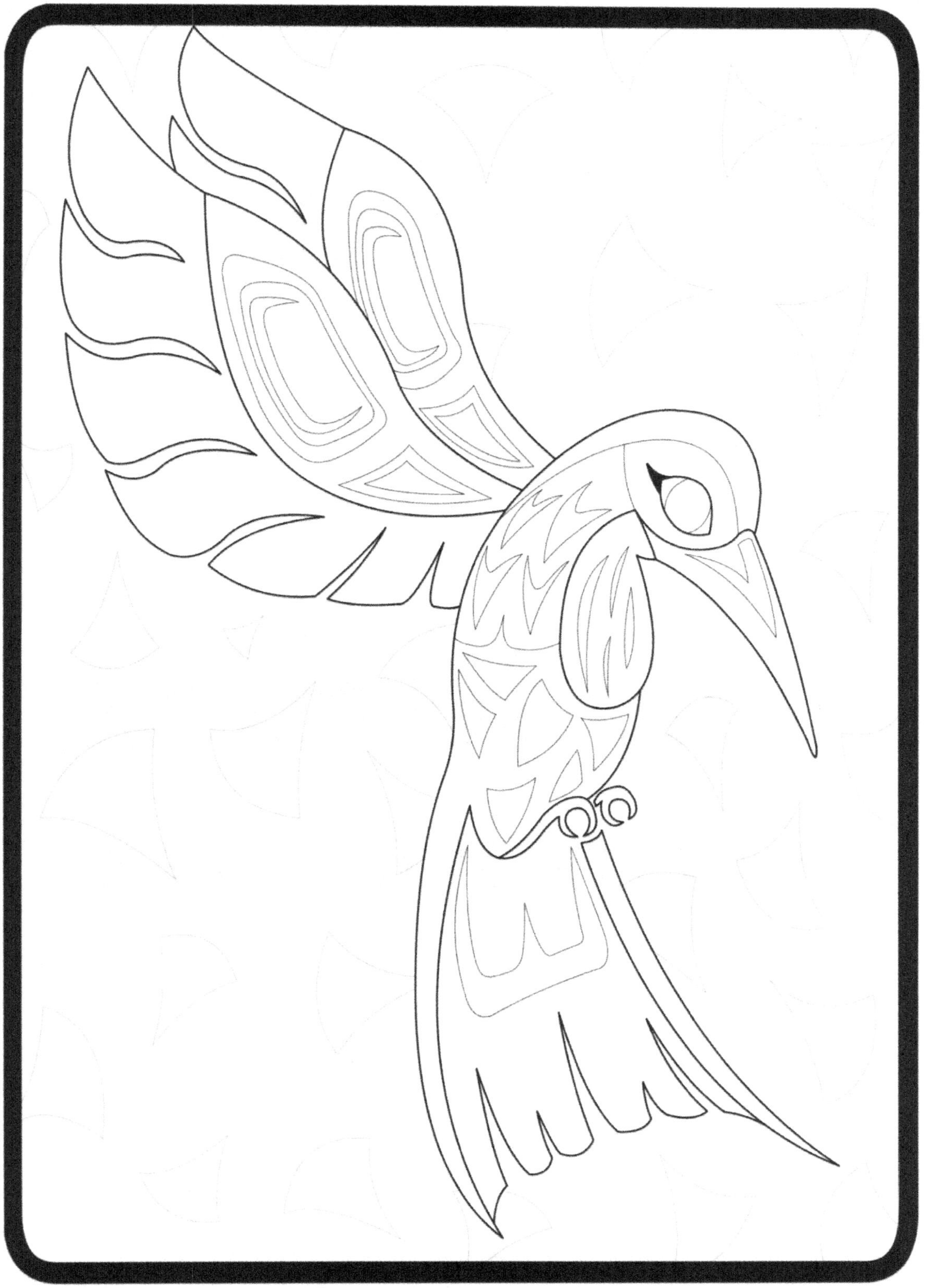

Baapaase

Red-Headed Woodpecker

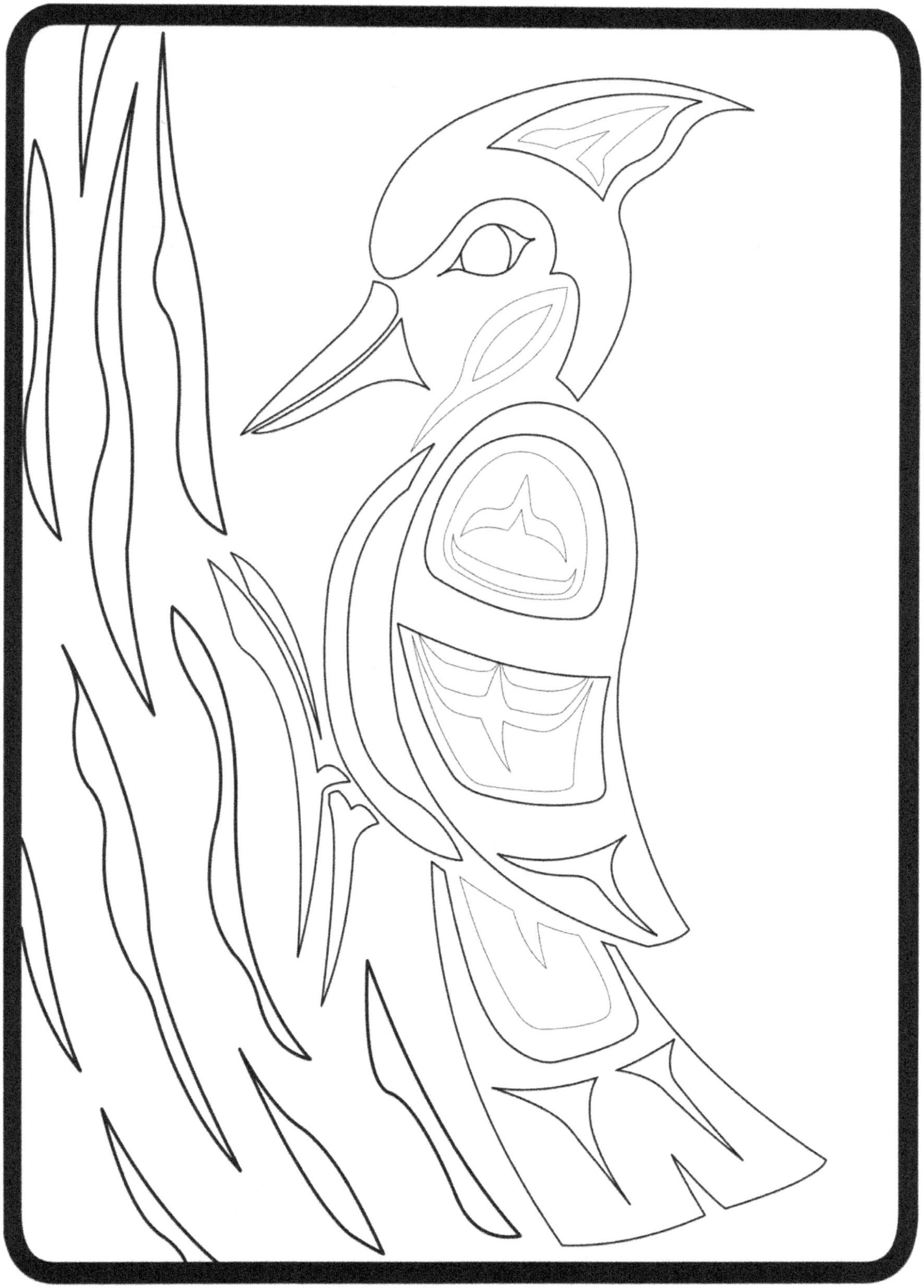

Gookooko'oo

Owl

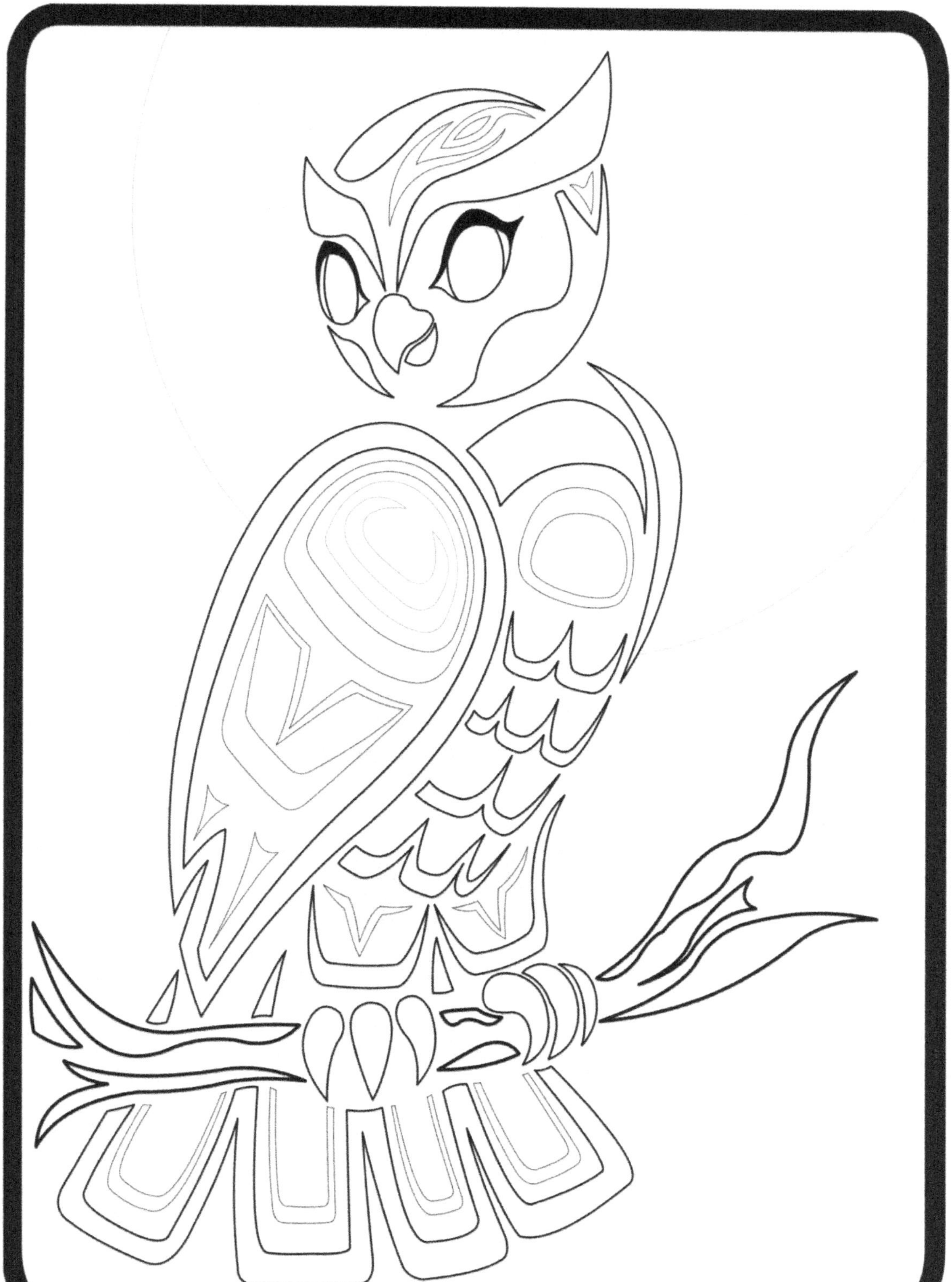

Aninaatig

Sugar Maple Tree

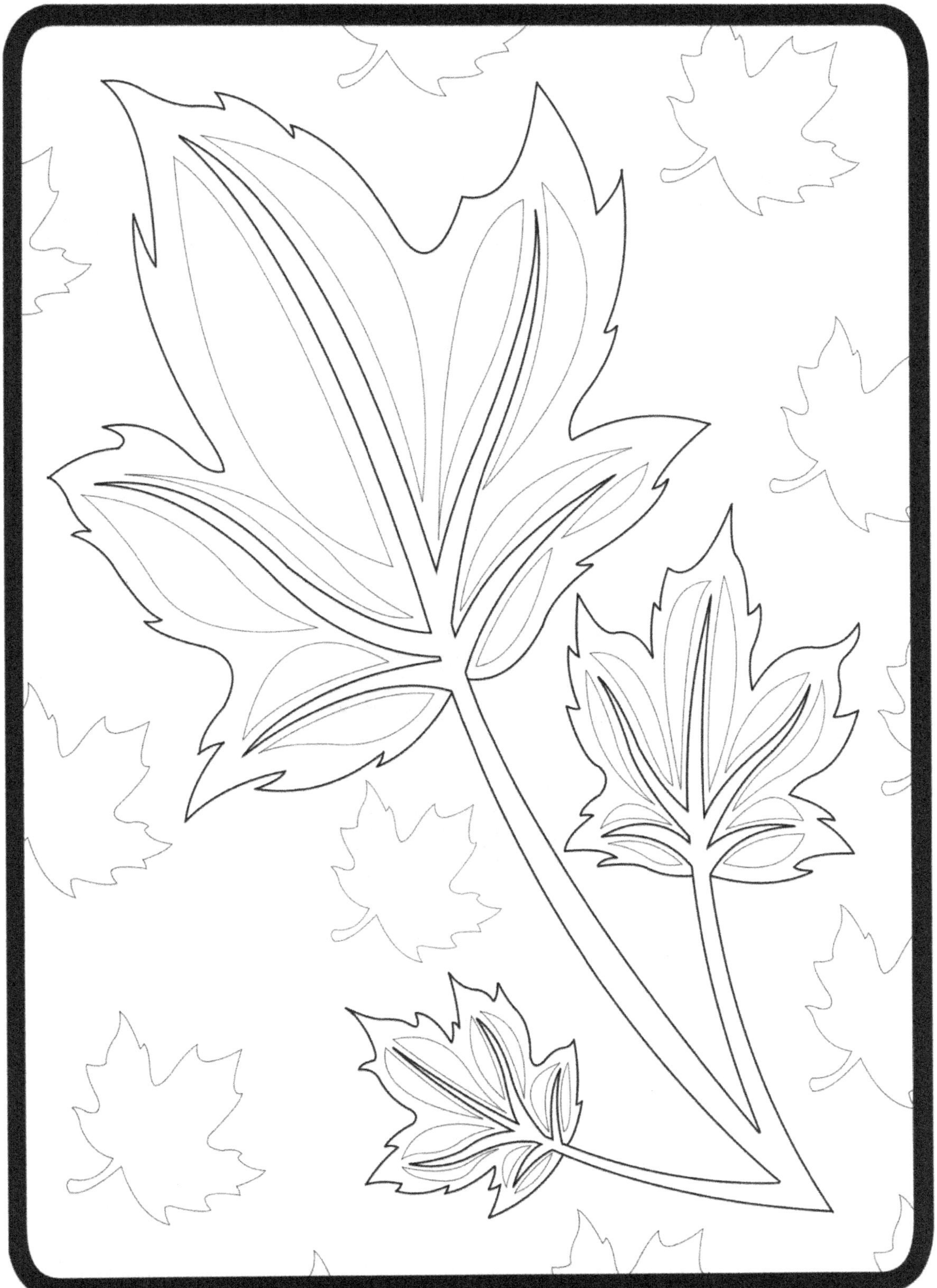

Gisheekandug

Cedar Tree

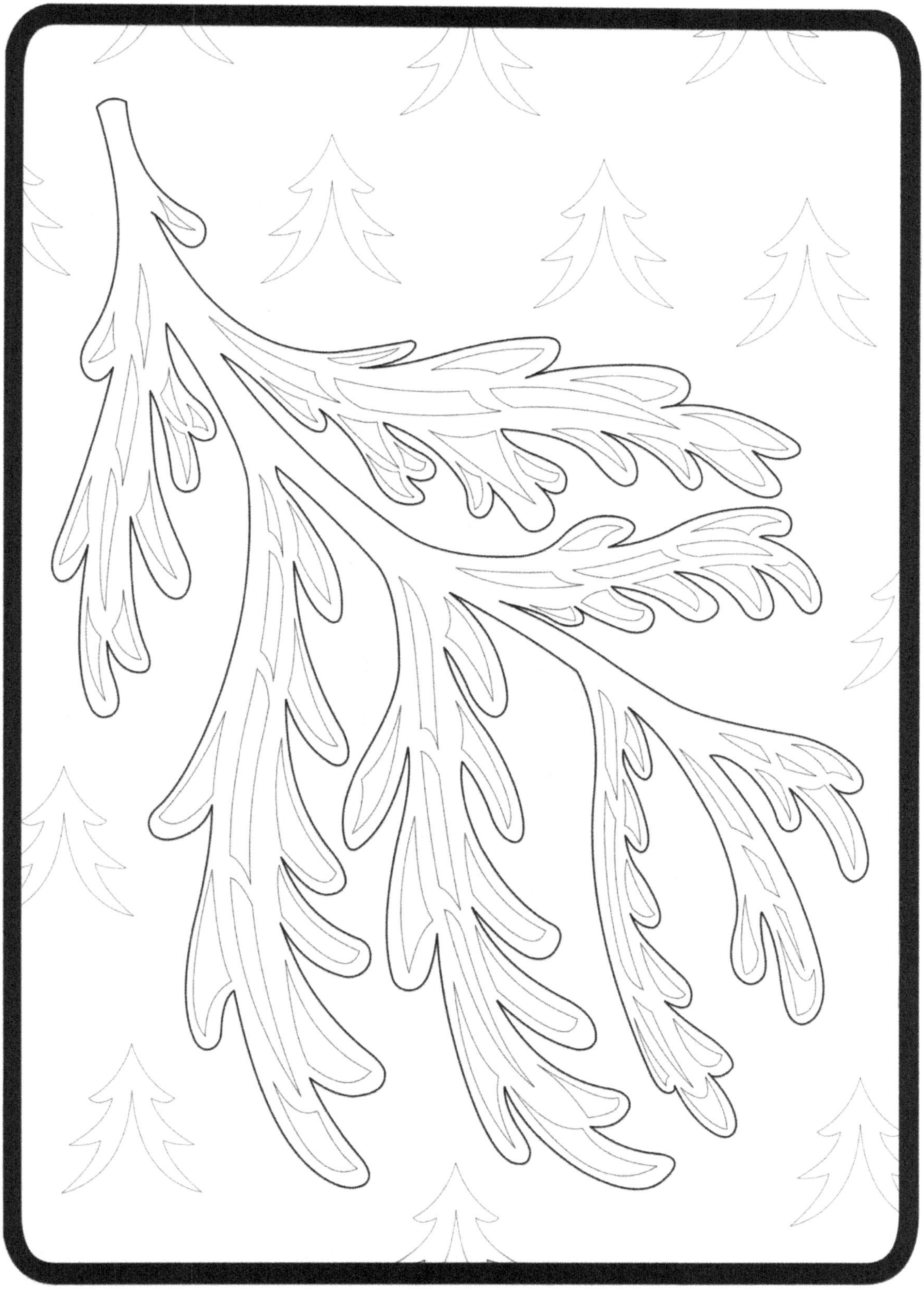

Miskwaabiimizh

Red-Osier Dogwood

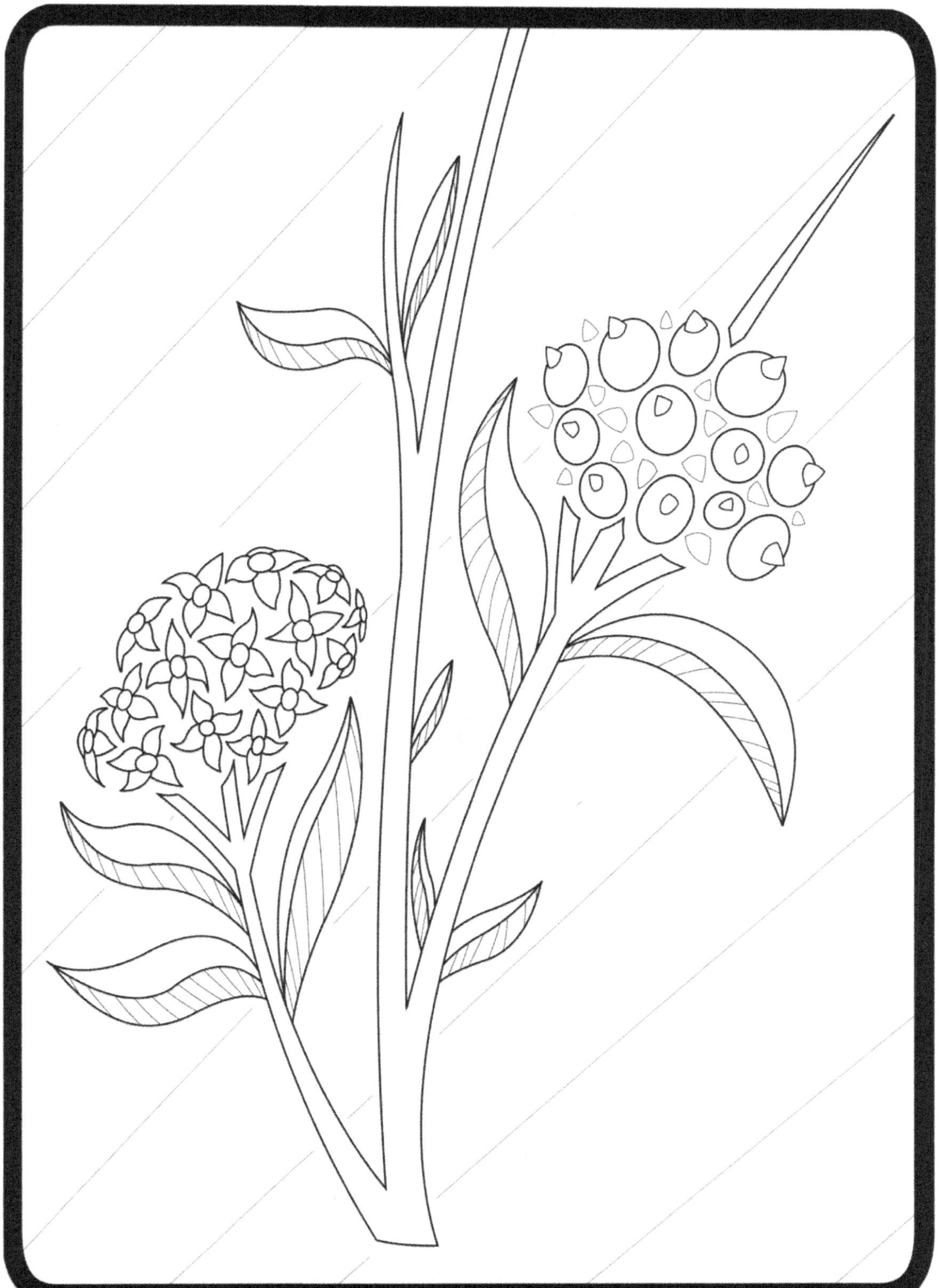

Aniibiimin

Juneberry

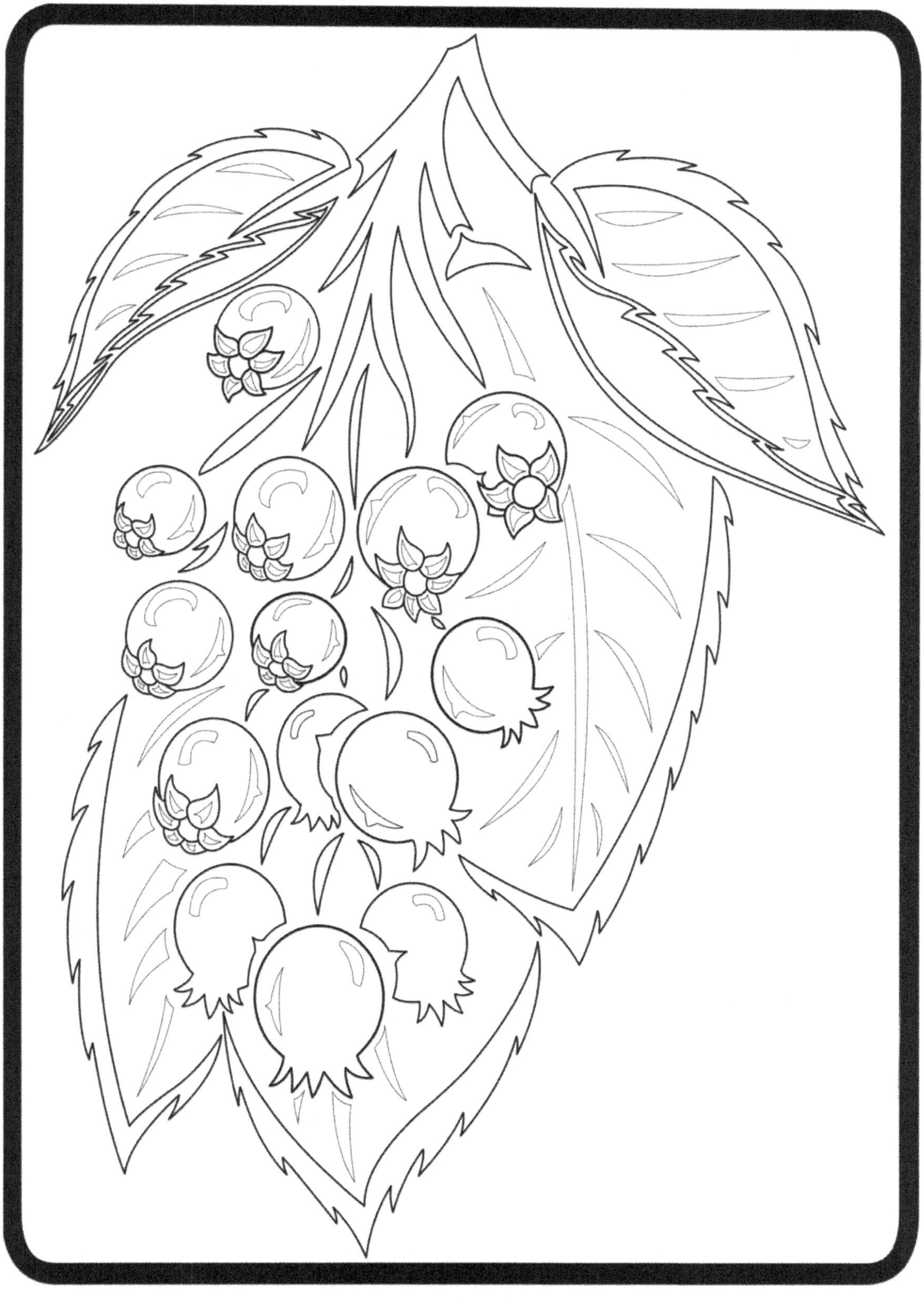

Odatagaagomin

Thimbleberry

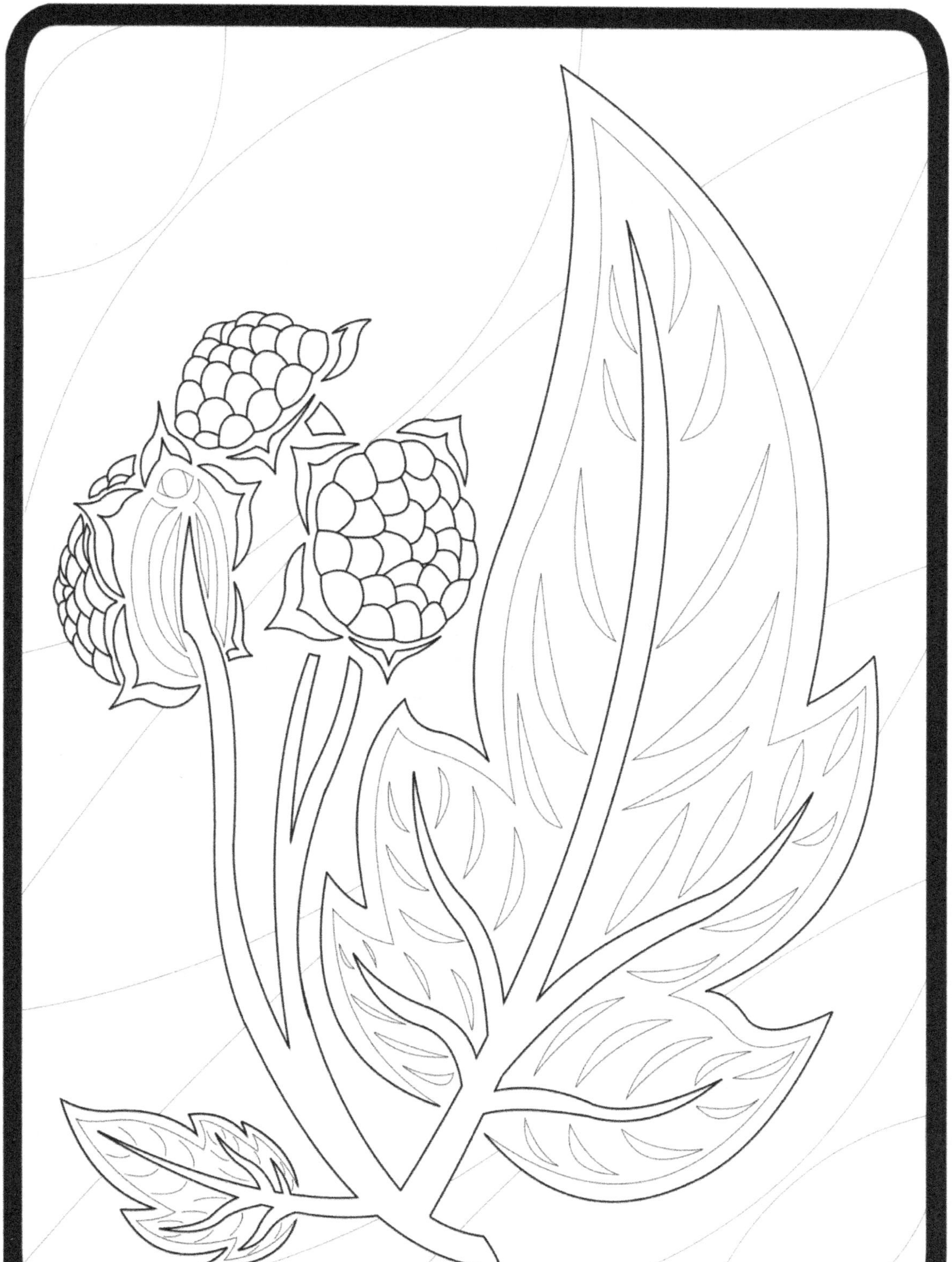

Miinan

Blueberry

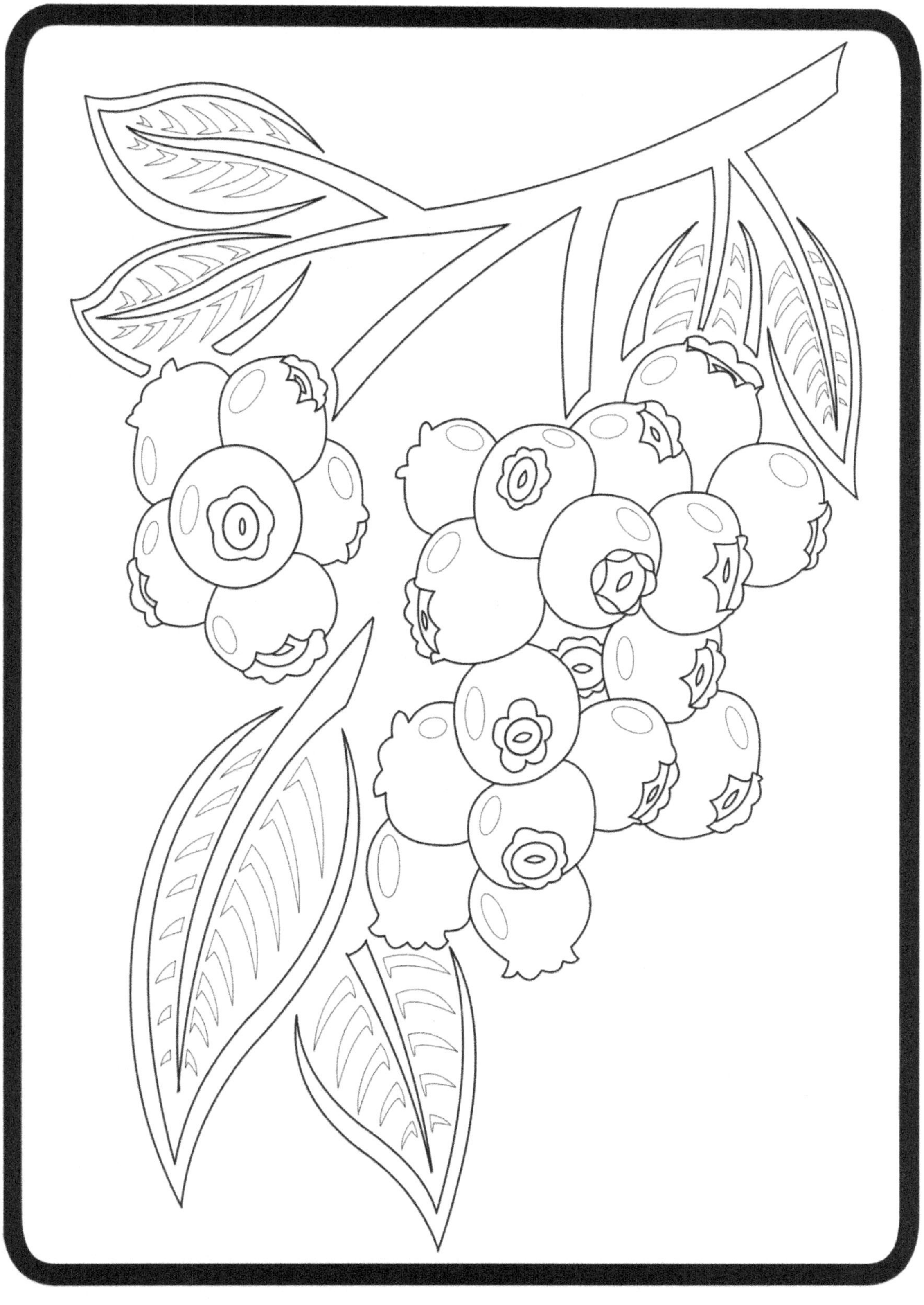

Ode'imin

Strawberry

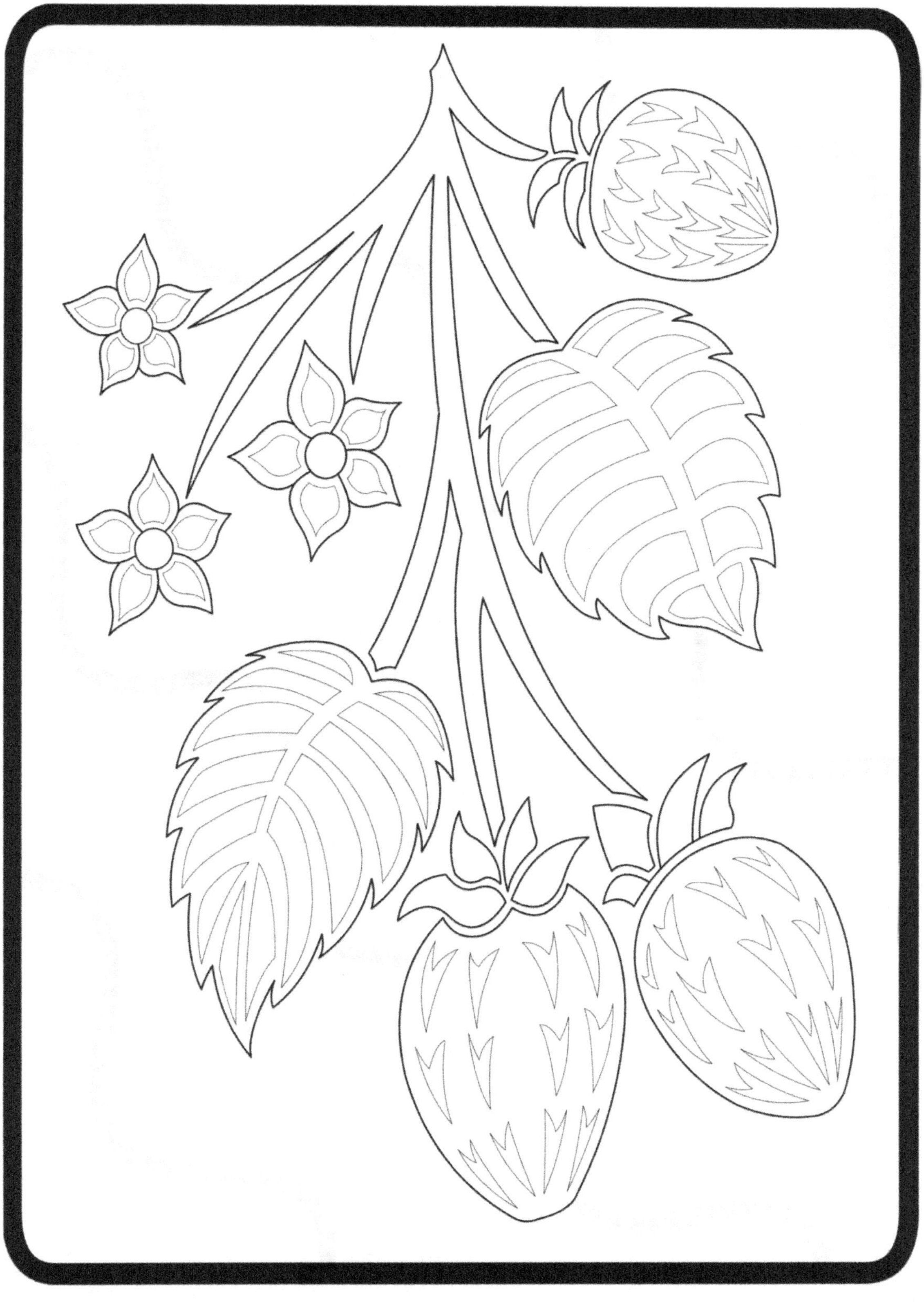

Apuk'we

Common Cattail

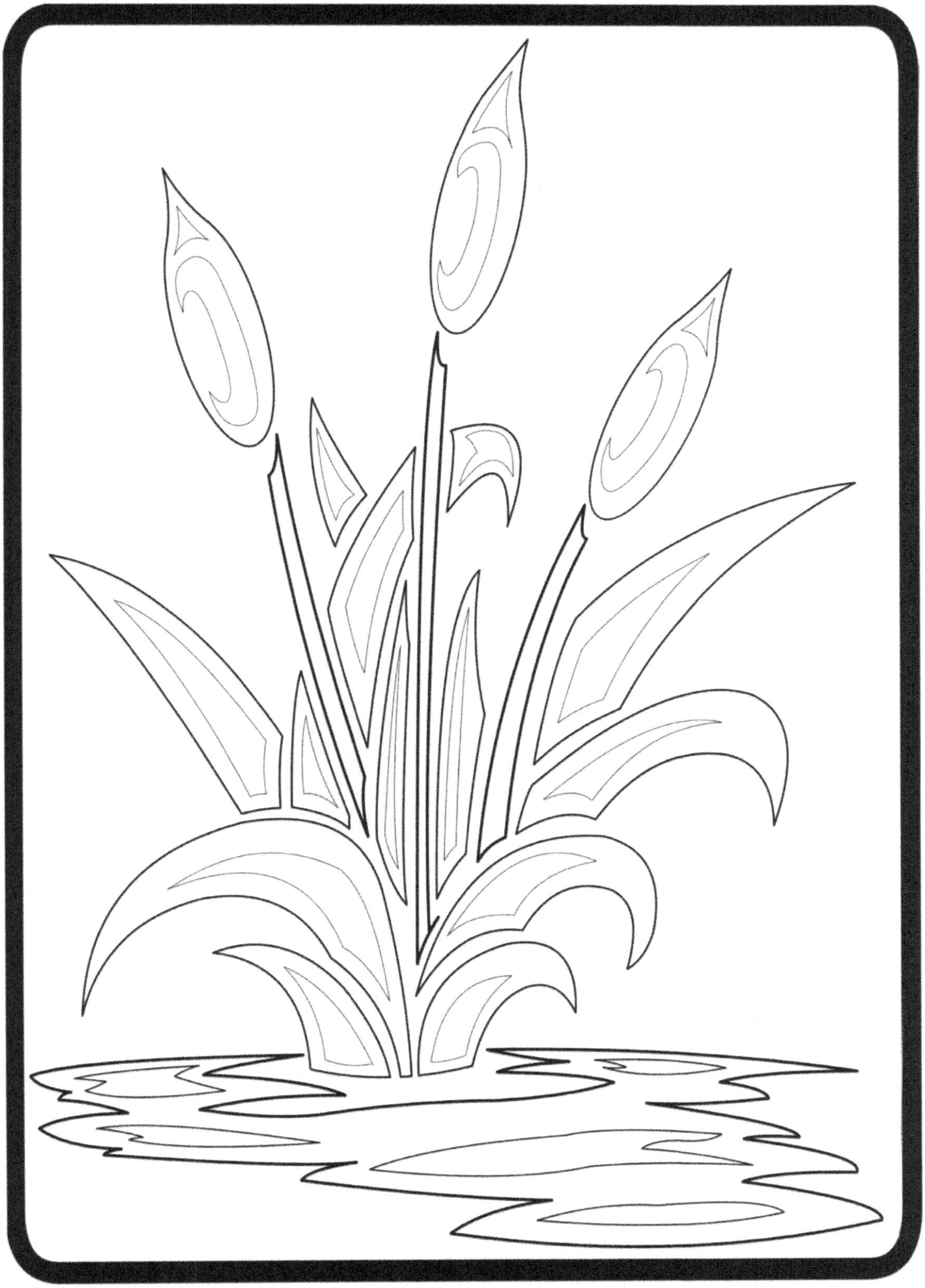

Dodoshaabo-jiibik

Dandelion

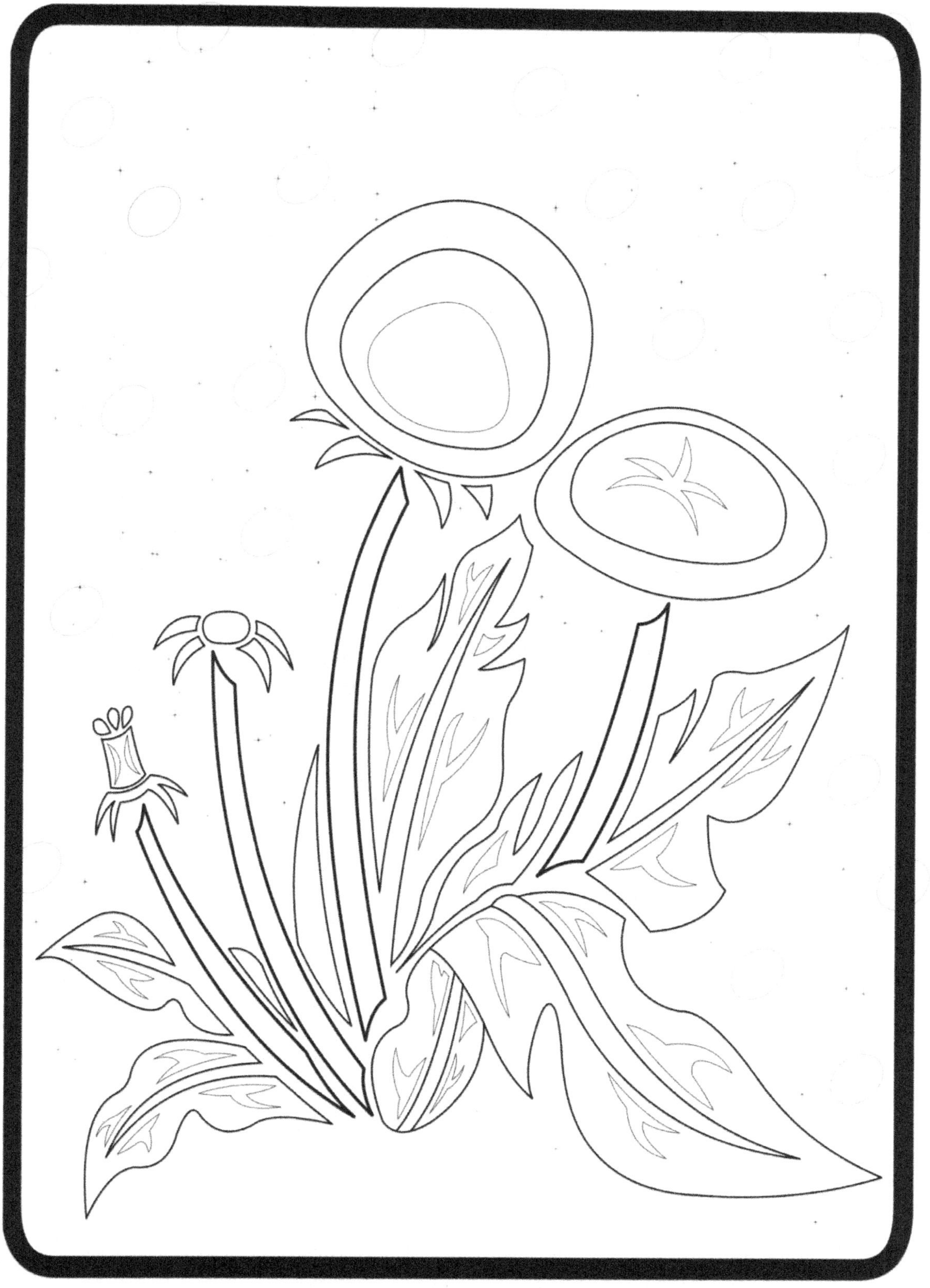

Waabigwan

Flower

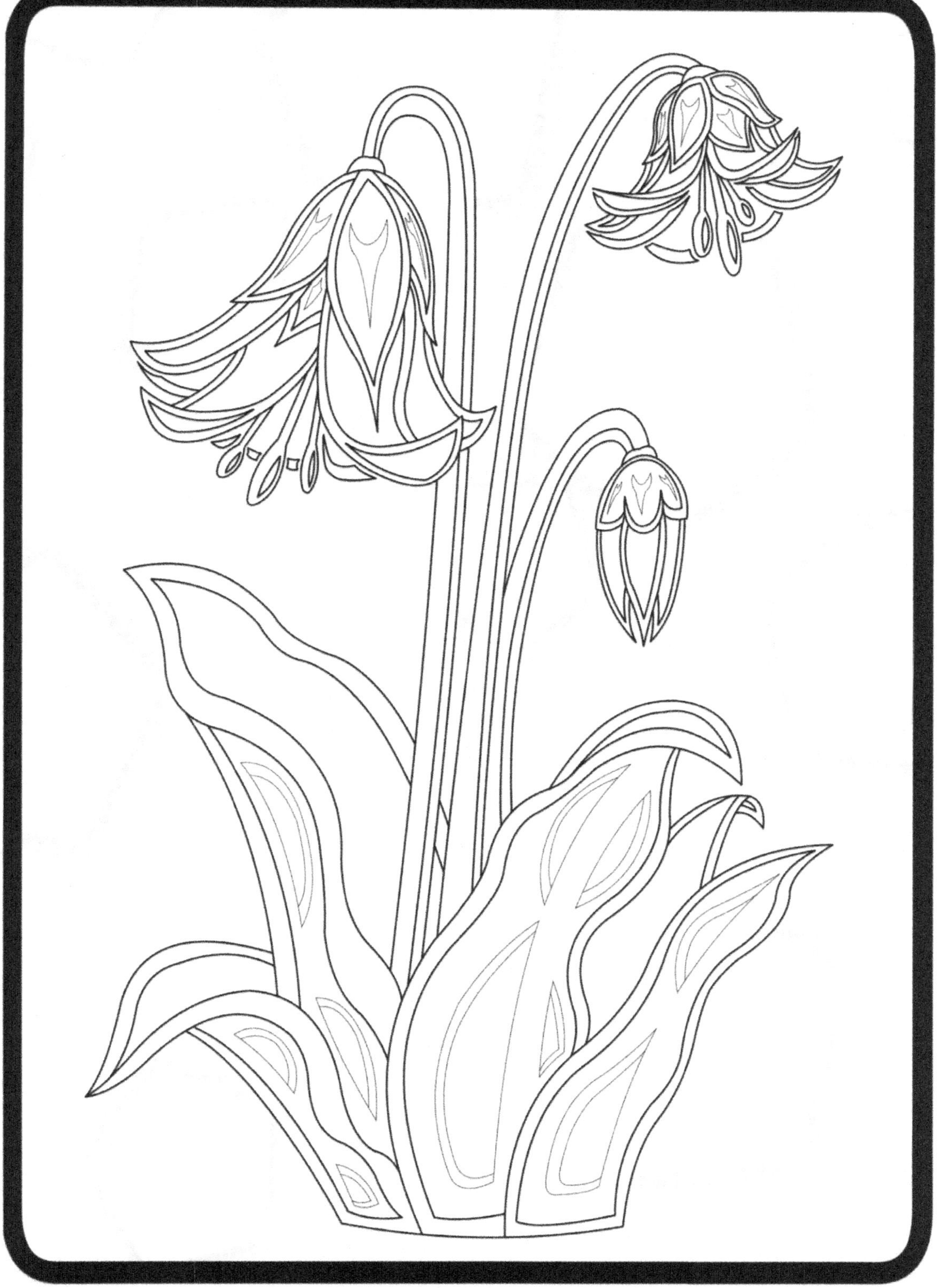

Each vowel is given below along with a phonetic transcription, Ojibwe words containing it, and one or more English words containing roughly equivalent sounds.
The letters standing for the sounds focused on are in bold.

Ojibwe Letter	Phonetic	Ojibwe Examples	English Equivalents
a	[ə]~[ʌ]	**a**gim - 'count someone!' n**a**m**a**dabi - 'sits down' baashkizig**a**n - 'gun'	**a**bout
aa	[a:]	**aa**gim - 'snowshoe' m**aa**j**aa** - 'goes away'	f**a**ther
e	[e:]~[ɛ:]	**e**mikwaan - 'spoon' aw**e**n**e**n - 'who' anishinaab**e** - 'person, ojibwe'	caf**é**
i	[I]	**i**n**i**ni- ' man' maw**i** - 'cries'	p**i**n
ii	[i:]	n**ii**n - 'I' goog**ii** - 'dives'	s**ee**n
o	[o]~[U]	**o**zid - 'someone's foot' an**o**kii - 'works' nib**o** - 'dies, is dead'	**o**bey b**oo**k
oo	[o:]~[u:]	**oo**dena - 'town' an**oo**kii - 'hires' g**oo**n - 'snow' bimibat**oo** - 'runs along'	b**oa**t b**oo**t

Nasal vowels are indicated by writing the appropriate basic vowel followed by **nh**. Before a **y** or a glottal stop ' the **h** may be omitted in writing. There are no direct English equivalents.

Ojibwe Letter	Phonetic	Ojibwe Examples
aanh	[ã:]	banajaanh - 'nestling'
enh	[ẽ:]~[ɛ̃:]	nisayenh - 'my older brother'
iinh	[ĩ:]	awesiinh - 'wild animal' agaashiinyi, agaashiinhyi - '(someone) is small'
oonh	[õ:]~[ũ:]	giigoonh - 'fish'

For more information on how to pronounce individual words please refer to The Ojibwe People's Dictionary at https://ojibwe.lib.umn.edu/

Ojibwe

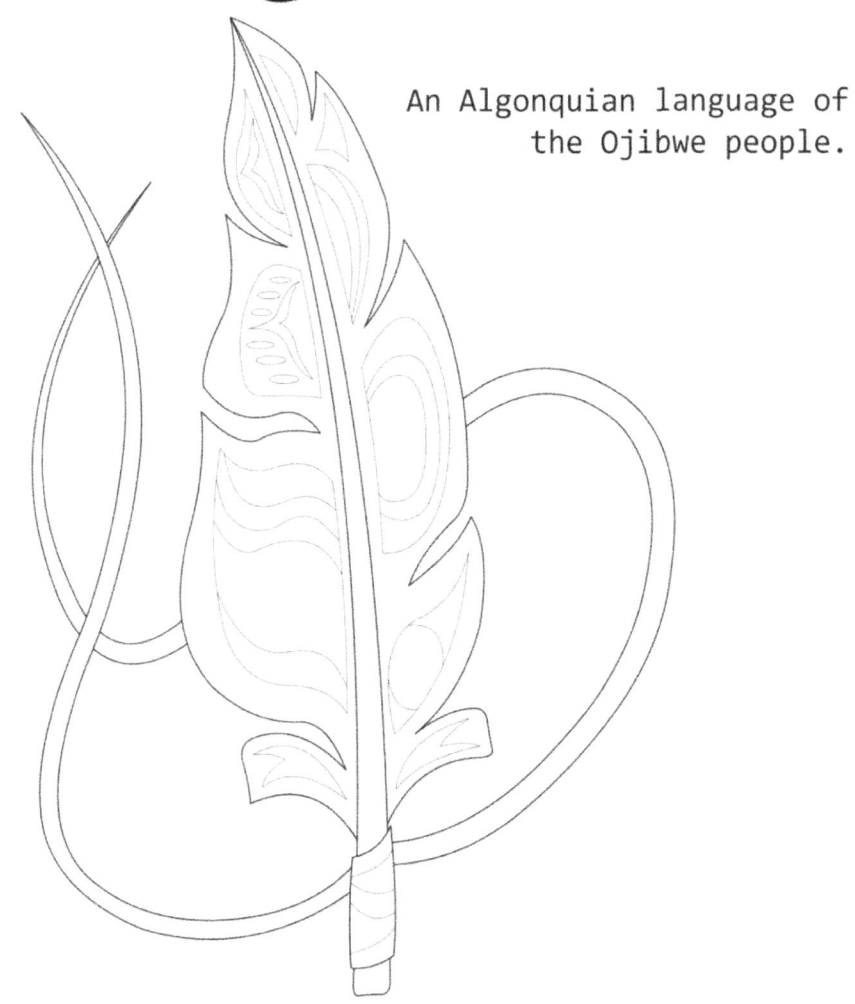

An Algonquian language of the Ojibwe people.

If you wish to support or check out other products by this artist please visit
https://ko-fi.com/kendrahowlandartscroll

Made in the USA
Monee, IL
23 April 2021